Dedicated to the future of 'the wide brown land'.

I Love A Sunburnt Country

Contents

Dorothea Mackellar Memorial Poetry Competition

My Country

The love of field and coppice,
Of green and shaded lanes,
Of ordered woods and gardens
Is running in your veins.
Strong love of grey-blue distance,
Brown streams and soft dim skies,
I know but cannot share it,
My love is otherwise.

I love a sunburnt country,
A land of sweeping plains,
Of ragged mountain ranges,
Of droughts and flooding rains;
I love her far horizons,
I love her jewel-sea,
Her beauty and her terror —
The wide brown land for me!

The tragic ringbarked forests,
Stark white beneath the moon,
The sapphire misted mountains,
The hot gold hush of noon,
Green tangle of the brushes
Where lithe lianas coil,
And orchids deck the tree tops
And ferns the crimson soil.

Core of my heart, my country!
Her pitiless blue sky,
When sick at heart around us
We see the cattle die —
But then the grey clouds gather
And we can bless again
The drumming of any army,
The steady soaking rain.

Core of my heart, my country!
Land of the Rainbow Gold,
For flood and fire and famine
She pays us back threefold,
Over the thirsty paddocks,
Watch, after many days,
The filmy veil of greenness
That thickens as we gaze.

An opal-hearted country,
A wilful lavish land —
All you who have not loved her,
You will not understand —
Though earth holds many splendours,
Wherever I may die,
I know to what brown country
My homing thoughts will fly.

DOROTHEA MACKELLAR O.B.E. (1885–1968) had a deep love for her country, which inspired her to write about the nature and moods of the Australian landscape. She wrote 'My Country' after witnessing the break of a prolonged drought while staying at her family's country property near Gunnedah.

FOREWORD

I first heard Dorothea Mackellar's famous poem a few years after settling in Australia when our eldest boy proudly recited 'My Country' on his way home from school. The poem immediately appealed to me as it so vividly described the sharp contrasts in this big country we had already called home. Soon I discovered that – apart from 'Waltzing Matilda' (the lyrics of which I found rather mysterious) – 'My Country' was practically the only popular expression of love for Australia. Furthermore, there seemed to be a certain shyness about publicly displaying patriotic feelings. I found this lack of enthusiasm hard to understand, as I was born in a country where abundant flag-waving and singing of patriotic songs were part of everyday life. Furthermore, like other Australians by choice, I often had to justify our naturalisation . . . and in doing so, soon found many reasons to sing and wave the flag about: I relished in the wide open spaces, stood in awe of the unbelievable riches in natural resources, was absorbed in the majestic and sometimes forboding beauty of this, our new country, and deeply admired the courage and endurance of the early pioneers.

For a while Dorothea and her poem disappeared into the background until many years later when our family moved from Sydney to the country. There I found that the poet I had long admired, used to spend most of her country holidays on the family property *Kurrumbede*, just outside the town of Gunnedah. This was her 'wide brown land'! Many older residents still remembered Dorothea and her brothers, Malcolm and Eric. I asked to see her memorial (responding to an old continental impulse) to be told that local attempts to honour the poet after her death in 1968 had failed.

I felt a great urge to take up the challenge to erect a Dorothea Mackellar memorial, especially after I became involved in organising the Australia Day celebrations in Gunnedah. A statue of the poet who first publicly expressed love for her Country would be an inspiration! A small fund-raising committee was formed and with the help of the media, Dorothea and her poem were rediscovered . . . for by that time the old practice of learning to recite 'My Country' had long been abandoned in schools.

The generation gap was slowly bridged. Memories were stirred and letters poured in from all over Australia with stories of the past, and with encouragement and donations to help erect a worthy memorial.

I sought to especially involve children in the project, to further rekindle the spirit behind the poem, and acquired permission to conduct a NSW Schools Appeal which raised $3000, representing 10 per cent of the total cost of erecting the life-sized bronze statue. It was unveiled on Australia Day 1983 by the contemporary poet, Rosemary Dobson.

The following year the first Dorothea Mackellar Memorial Poetry Competition For Schools was conducted 'to encourage young Australians to adequately express their views on Home, Country and the Environment'. The shoestring budget restricted the competition to NSW schools only, but having in mind that Dorothea Mackellar wrote her poem for the whole of our country, it was soon decided to take the plunge and invite schools in all States and Territories to participate.

With financial assistance from the National Australia Day Council and operational support from all State and Territory Australia Day Councils, the competition has steadily grown into the largest of its kind in the world. I am proud to acknowledge that one of Australia's oldest leading companies, QBE Insurance, is now the national sponsor of the competition so that potential for its further growth will be realised. The success of this project is due to so many people sharing my vision and being willing to support the concept which promotes the expression of love for our country and encourages creative writing. It also helps to foster a better understanding between young Australians from various backgrounds, who all live in such vastly different circumstances throughout our great continent.

It is a source of great joy and gratification to me that the ABC—an organisation with which I have been connected from time to time for many years—has published this documentary of views expressed by our younger generation.

I Love a Sunburnt Country will undoubtedly strengthen the bond created between participating schools and encourage others to join in. I hope the anthology will enthuse local communities to organise their own poetry festivals and I am sure that readers, young and old, will gain some wisdom and enjoyment from the sometimes serious, surprisingly philosophical and often humorous way in which the various topics have been treated.

MIKIE MAAS OAM

Published by ABC Books for the
AUSTRALIAN BROADCASTING
CORPORATION
GPO Box 9994 Sydney NSW 2001

First published 1993

National Library of Australia
Cataloguing-in-Publication entry
I love a sunburnt country: poems
from the Dorothea Mackellar
Memorial Poetry Competition for
Schools 1984-1992

ISBN 0 7333 0256 4.

1. Austalian poetry—20th century.
I. Australian Broadcasting
Corporation. II. Dorothea
Mackellar Memorial Poetry
Competition.

A821.308

Designed by Felicity Meyer
Cover painting by Jean Isherwood FRAS
'Ragged Mountain Range'
Set in 12/14½ Berkley Oldstyle by
Midland Typesetters, Maryborough
Printed and bound in Australia by
Australian Print Group,
Maryborough, Victoria

3.5-1695

1984

My Country

The Dorothea Mackellar Memorial was erected in 1983. As is indicated on the plaque, the Memorial was erected by 'the people of Australia, the children of New South Wales and the local community'. In 1984 the Memorial Trust established the perpetual phase of the project. *The Dorothea Mackellar Memorial Poetry Awards* consisted of the following prizes:

- an inscribed Dennis Adams statuette of the memorial
- Two hundred and fifty dollars cash and
- Free return travel and two nights accommodation, to enable winners of the Primary and Secondary Sections to receive the Awards in Gunnedah on Australia Day.

The inaugural NSW Schools Poetry Competition was a great success with over eighty schools participating. The 300 poems written on the topic 'My Country' were judged by Rosemary Dobson, one of our leading contemporary poets who has since received the Order of Australia for her contribution to Literature, and Joan Phipson, award-winning author and member of the Literature Board of the Australia Council.

All entries were returned to the schools, together with a report containing the results and winning poems. All participants received a signed 'Certificate of Appreciation' for their contribution.

SECONDARY SECTION

FIRST

AUSTRALIA

Beneath the rock that rises from the sand,
The muffled footsteps of a ghostly band
Sink softly in this fierce and ancient land:
Dreamtime Australia.

The dust-cloud rests upon the open plain.
The sun shines down on heads of golden grain.
Mirages form and melt, then form again:
Inland Australia.

Age-old mountains, reaching for the sky,
Gaze down on rivers roaring from on high,
While clear and chiming comes the bellbird's cry:
Scenic Australia.

To lie on sunlit sands and watch the sea . . .
And know within my heart that I am free.
There is no other home than this for me:
This is Australia.

Desireé Jurgs, aged 15
Narrabri High School
Narrabri NSW

Desireé in 1984

PRIMARY SECTION

FIRST

Our Small Part of Australia—Tingha

Not an echo breaks the stillness,
Riding home from droving cattle.
Ragged bark on dying trees.
The cattle now are gone.
The wind breaks the stillness
As the sun goes slowly down.

As I put my horse away
Thunder cracks overhead;
Lightning flashes and
The rain begins to pour.
No longer can I work.
The floods arrive —
Sixteen more days till it's done.

The days go by.
The floods recede.
Bridges are down.
The crops are ruined.

Tingha is a strong town.
It's not for the weak.
Floods, fires or drought —
We can defeat them all.
Whatever it is:
We are strong enough.

Toni Cameron, aged 11
Tingha Public School
Tingha NSW

Toni in 1984

SECONDARY SECTION

Aussie Child

Catch the clouds, sunburned child,
Reach and learn to stand.
Walk towards your destiny,
Stop clinging to the sand.

Many-mothered pupil, grow
Strong in freedom, learn to run!
Wildness, newness . . . all is yours:
Gifts of the relentless sun.

Nation, who now owns the land
Still in childhood near the shore:
Top the spirit of this place,
Rise from those who went before.

Greg Waters, aged 17
St Joseph's High School
Aberdeen NSW

PRIMARY SECTION

My Country

Fat cows, woolly sheep
Quietly grazing near the creek.
Sunny days and bright blue sky,
Where the eagle loves to fly.
I gallop with my pony friend
To where the box trees sway and bend.
Little lambs skip, buck and play
And scatter quickly from my way.
My outback home, so wide and free,
Is where I always hope I'll be.
I quietly turn my pony's head
And wander slowly home to bed.

Rebecca Brown, aged 6
School of the Air
Broken Hill NSW

1985

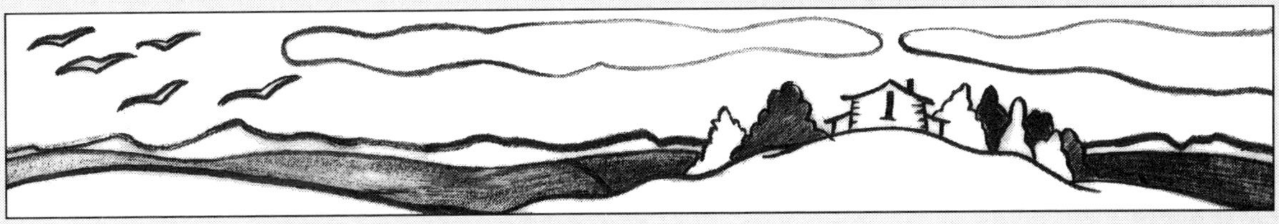

The Place Where I Live

Four hundred poems were received from 200 participating Schools—an amazing increase from the previous year considering this was only the second year the competition had been conducted. National media attention and in particular, the continued publicity given to the competition by Ian McNamara on the ABC program 'Australia All Over', prompted Schools from Queensland, the ACT, Victoria and South Australia to submit their pupils' views on the 1985 Subject 'The Place Where I Live'. As a result, serious thoughts were given to making the competition a national contest in future.

Many entrants took great care in illustrating their work which triggered the introduction of the Anne Bell Prize for the best presented poem. The Prize consisted of a trophy, a book autographed by poet/artist Anne Bell, and twenty-five dollars cash.

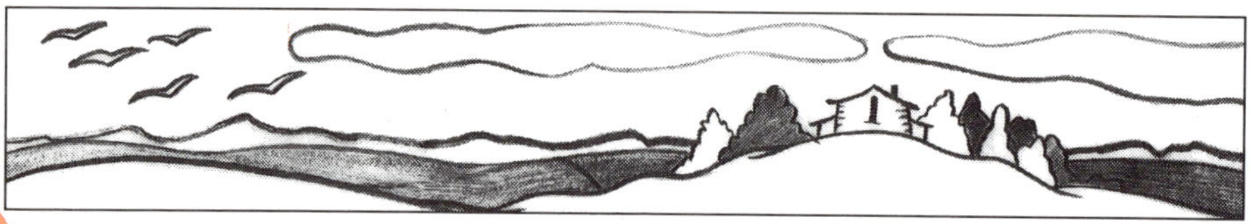

SECONDARY SECTION

FIRST

THE CHALLENGE OF MY HOME

Years before man's footfall upon the earth was heard,
Before there came to break the silence, call of beast or bird . . .
A deep and brooding stillness settled on this ancient land
And the only mark upon it was the movement of God's hand.
Shrouded then in mystery;
A life before our history;
A land that had so much to give,
This place where now the lucky live.

As it waited for the native who would make this land his own,
This mighty country nurtured here the peace which God had sown.
Its raw and rugged mountains stood as guardians to the plains
And unseen caverns formed below, carved out by teeming rains.
A place of beauty hidden deep,
Awakening from quiet sleep:
Rocks, stars and trees presenting here
The Dreamtime truths to draw us near.

That untouched land has altered much with centuries gone by:
Cities cling where forests grew . . . and planes command the sky.
From mines and soil the riches come to bring prosperity,
But my country's greatest riches are the ones that she gives, free.
Her peace, strength and serenity
Stand high among her gifts to me.
But now she asks: 'What will you give
To me, this place in which you live?'

Desireé Jurgs, aged 16
New England Girls' High
Armidale NSW

Desireé in 1992

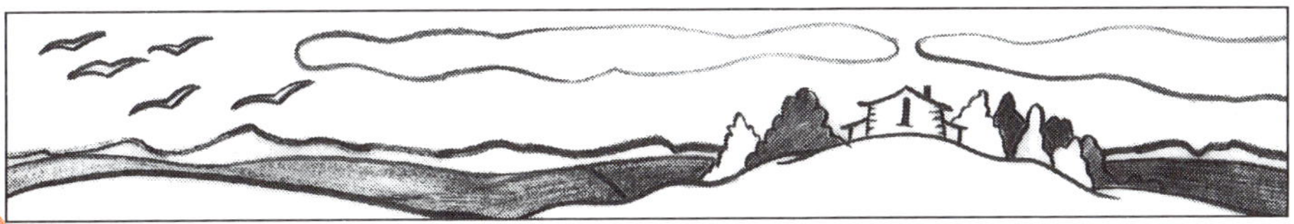

PRIMARY SECTION

FIRST

THE PLACE WHERE I LIVE

I like the sounds at my place —
The foolish talk of the peewee,
The gentle swish of a stick falling,
The high-noted trill of a thrush
And the lusty chuckle of the kookaburras.

I like the silence at my place —
The breeze pondering by,
A mopoke flying swiftly through the night air;
The depth of space
And the clouds standing guard on the hill.

I like the movement at my place —
A plover chasing a magpie off its territory,
A hawk steadily hovering about the corn-patch,
A crayfish quietly slipping along the creek bank
And the dam rippling to the slow rhythm of the wind.

I like the stillness at my place —
A cormorant perched on a snag drying its wings,
A goanna basking in the sun,
Some weeds entwining themselves
And the trees on a hot summer's day.

I like to smell at my place —
The fresh fragrance of the gumblossom
Wafting past my nose,
The leaflitter scent emerging from the ground,
The spicy odour of grass after it has been mown
And the clear air on a frosty morning.

I like to feel at my place —
A smooth warm fresh egg,
The tickly clover on my bare feet,
Dry soft sand by the creek
And the velvety coat of our house cow.

I like the place where I live.

Wayne in 1985

Wayne Allen, aged 10
Byabarra Public School
Byabarra NSW

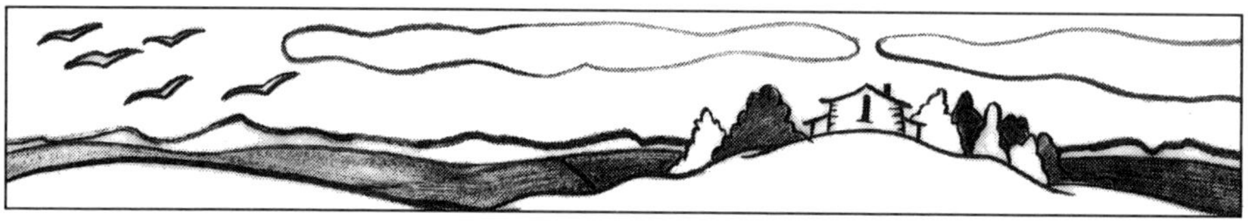

PRIMARY SECTION

THE FIGTREE REMEMBERS

The Figtree towers above the suburb that bears its name.
'It is wise' they say, 'It has seen things change.'
It is old. Older than the White men of Australia
And so it must hold deep secrets, yet untold.
So what are its memories?

It saw the first Australians, the brown people.
The spirit of the Figtree watched over them
As beneath the sunset in the late evening
The abundant food was shared among the tribe.
Then, enveloped in the warm night air,
Men and women sang in Dharawal and clapped in rhythm.
And before long, the familiar droning sound
Of the Didgeridoo joined their chant.

Beneath the stars and glistening moon
And the looming shadow of the mountain Keira,
As the great orange fire crackled and blazed fiercely,
Men told the secrets of their spirit ancestors.
These secrets the Figtree guards.

The Figtree watched as the white men came.
Men with pale faces, holding long fire sticks.
Spirits, bad spirits from distant Dreamtime legends
As ancient as the emerald hills on the horizon.
The white men took the Mother land and felled the trees,
Trying to transform the grey-green of the wilderness
Into the orderly fields of England.

And — in a way — the land was tamed.
Settlements dotted the mountains' folds and fringed the coastal plains.
The Aborigines, displaced, melted away into the hills.
Where once were tribal grounds, only bones of the past remain.
For its dead, the Figtree mourns.

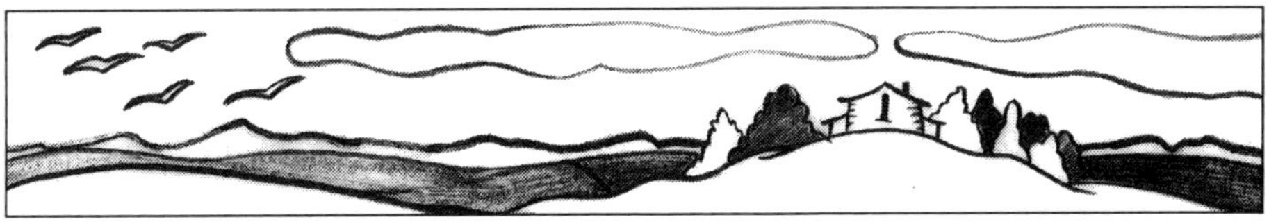

Today the world has changed.
The Figtree stands amidst the bustling city Wollongong
Above the noisy highway, where the traffic roars.
In the hazy distance the steelworks fume
Thick grey clouds of smoke, like an angry giant.
From the clustered houses children run with happy laughter
To soften the Figtree's lonely heart.

Still the Figtree stands, tall and strong:
A monument to the people of the past.
To the brown people who nursed the land
And to the white people who toiled to tame it.
These are the Figtree's memories.

Catriona Nagi, aged 11
Figtree Primary School
Figtree NSW

PRIMARY SECTION

THE PLACE WHERE I LIVE

Tall mountains touching the sky;
Rocks and trees just lie.
Running waterfalls tumbling over
Juicy grass with lots of clover.
Sunshowers brightening up
Filling our cup.
Furry soft moss clinging;
Notes of birds dinging.
A present to give
The place where I live.

Danny Tracey, aged 6
Comboyne Kinder
Comboyne NSW

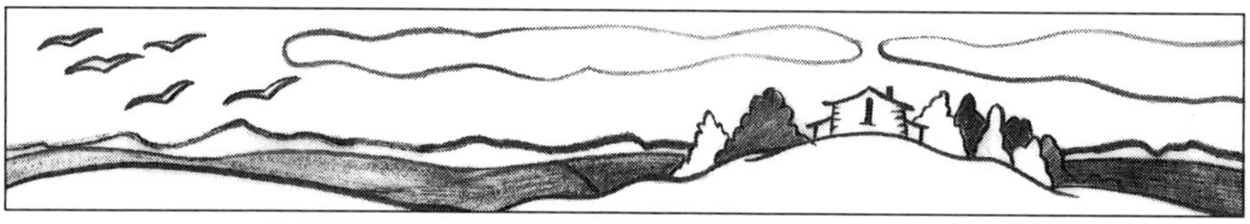

PRIMARY SECTION

It Gets Busy Where I Live

The sun is rising brightly on another busy day,
So hurry up! Get out of bed! No time to romp and play!
School is ever waiting and no matter how I try,
There always seems to be another set before my eye.
The radio is crackling with a lesson on the air,
I cannot hear it properly and I'm pulling out my hair!
The mathematics problems just never will come right
And my reading lesson nearly always ends up in a fight.

Mustering time is with us and Dad hasn't got a minute,
He's already killed our mutton but it's me who has to skin it!
The aeroplane is overhead: Dad's spotting scattered sheep
And now he's radioed to say 'tell Ben to bring the jeep.
Make him get a move on now, I need him right away
To gather up the tiny lambs, too young to walk all day.'
So bouncing through the bush I go, I know I'll be in trouble
If I don't do what Dad has said — and do it on the double!

In the noisy, dusty drafting yard I sort the sheep all day,
The shearers have been busy and there's wool to get away,
For up beside the wool shed the bales are piled up high,
The wool truck is arriving with a man who wants to buy.
I love to climb the 'wool-bale hill' and then just stand and stare
At the milling sheep, the barking dogs and busy scene down there.
But then Dad shouts 'Where's that boy gone, he's disappeared
from sight!
Get down and put the billy on or we'll be here all night!'

So once again I'm rushing round with lots of jobs to do
And I have to keep my school work up: that's most important too!
There's always something to be done and something waiting, yet
Tomorrow is another day, a busy one I'll bet.
It gets busy where I live. Sometimes there's not a minute
To laze around beside the pool, or wallow gaily in it.
But just the same I love it here amongst the grazing sheep,
Where families are important and peace is strong and deep.

Ben Brown, aged 10
School of the Air
Broken Hill NSW

1986

A Typical Australian

The competition was conducted on a national basis for the first time this year, attracting close to 600 entries. The topic 'A Typical Australian', originally set to embrace a wide variety of interpretations, was often treated narrowly . . . and for the first time the influence of the media on children's minds became apparent as hundreds of young poets described the beer-drinking, sloppy fat TV-watching 'Norm' as the 'typical' Australian! The Judges, looking for originality, power of observation, a sense of form and expressions of genuine feeling, thought highly of the poems that showed the writer had really thought about the subject . . . without succumbing to preconceived ideas.

Great support was received from Departments of Education in every State and Territory, resulting in submissions by schools from all over Australia.

The 'Grannie Award' for the 'Under 8' Group was added as an incentive for the very young. The winner — though still eligible for the main Primary Award — received a trophy and a book, autographed by 'Grannie'.

Entries were returned with the report for the last time as this proved to be a near impossible task . . . and hand-writing the certificates became a 'labour of love'!

Dorothea Mackellar Memorial Poetry Competition

SECONDARY SECTION

FIRST

THE TYPICAL AUSTRALIAN

Yes Darling/Sweetheart/Dear/Love/Pet . . .
Her thick, maternal tree-arms
Will encompass anything
As she waits behind the fly-wire door.
She has spread her full and sunburnt love,
Her great expansive love
Among many.

Her sound, omniscient eyes —
Those soft, damp and giving petalled eyes,
Those hard, threatening, dry rock eyes —
Change with the sun;
Change with the moon;
Change with the stars
And reveal the space of her time.

For she has lived a long, long time;
A dream time;
A dancing story old old gone time.
And she has been naked and young;
And she has bounced her black feet
Red among the dust.
And she has cut her white feet
Red upon a rock.
And all have lived.
And all have died
Upon her open face.

She has felt
The generations of falling leaves
Fall lightly upon her flesh.
And she has sucked from the air
All she has needed
To nourish and home those of her body
In perpetual procreation.

She is clothed in floral dress,
Adorned with paints of rainbow colours;
Her head embellished with a multitude of merry wigs;
Her fingers, with rings, dazzling in the sun.

She has been celebrated with movement and voice;
Used and drained by drilling bores;
And lets lap upon her shores
The green tongues that lick from the sea that surrounds her:
For she knows she will not drown.

Michelle Ryan, aged 17
Avila College
Waverley Vic

PRIMARY SECTION

FIRST

AN AUSTRALIAN DAY FOR A KANGAROO

The break of day.
The beautiful pink in the sky.
A magpie calls to wake life:
I feel born again
To be free with the breeze
That tugs at my hair
And mingles with the leaves.

From between the bushes,
From the olive green,
A kangaroo appears.
His head jerks upward.
I wonder what he's seen.

Then gradually he continues eating,
Still listening, keen —
When once more
He's startled again.
This time he doesn't stay.
His powerful tan tail
Heaves him off — and he's away:
The beauty! The speed!
Gracefully he bounds
Over the spiny shrubs.
Silently . . . no sound.
Again he stops — motionless.
Smells the fresh scent
Of the gum leaves.
The bright sun lent
Its warm rays
And glistens on the kangaroo's
golden hair.
It seems as if he's searching
Here by himself.

And as the sun goes down
Behind the scorching horizon,
In one effortless bound
He's gone.
A kookaburra laughs
To end an Australian day.

Linda in 1986

Linda Kennedy, aged 12
Ross Park Primary
Alice Springs NT

GRANNIE AWARD

A Typical Australian

Other kids at school
Sometimes laugh at me.
They say my eyes are different,
But they must be OK: they see!

My mum, she comes from Leyte:
Her island in the sun.
We went there for a holiday
And I had lots of fun.

My Dad works in the bush.
He is big and rough and tough.
But he really loves me,
I guess that is enough.

I ask Dad, was I Typical?
Whatever that may be.
He said: my son, a more typical Australian
I have yet to see.

I know that I am lucky:
I have lots of friends
Who don't care about my eyes
That bend up at the ends.

Richard Gudgeon, aged 6
Gulgong Public School
Gulgong NSW

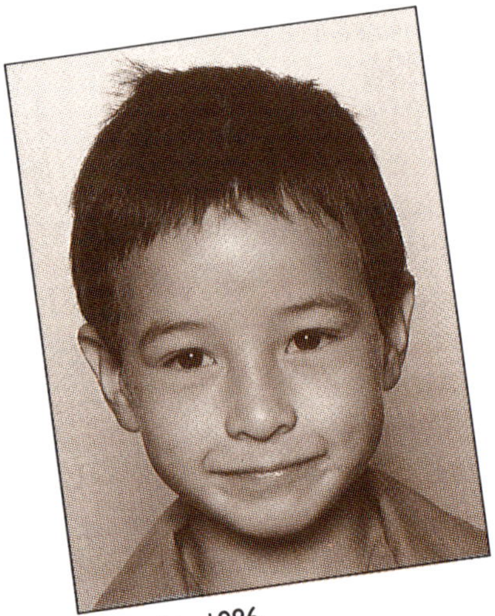

Richard in 1986

PRIMARY SECTION

A TYPICAL AUSTRALIAN

My typical Australian is
— and you may ask me why —
Not a boozer or a gambler,
But the old BLOW FLY.

You can meet him in the Parliament,
You can meet him in the slums;
You will find him at the beach or
Out among the gums.

You can travel the whole of Australia
From Perth to Gundagai . . .
And as soon as you get your tucker out:
There's that old BLOW FLY.

Mark Blake, aged 11
Ballarat Primary School
Ballarat Vic

PRIMARY SECTION

TYPICAL AUSTRALIAN

To be a real Australian
Is to be a dinky-di;

Also to like tomato sauce
And the old meat pie.

To be a real Australian
Is to say 'How're you going mate',

Or to have a vegemite sandwich
On an old glass plate.

To be a real Australian
Is not to point the bone,

But try to live on the smell
Of an oil rag or icecream cone.

To be a real Australian
Is to wish every-body luck

And hope the next budget will
Increase our deflated buck!

Amelia Scicluna, aged 10
St Jude's Primary School
Holder ACT

Only An Australian

Only an Australian
Would go to the football
So he can suck a pie.

Only he can abuse his mates
And get away with it.

Only a Yobbo
Can swear in public
And be accepted.

Only a Norm
Can call South Africans: 'Racists!'
Then slang off at Aborigines.

Only a Greenie
Can cuddle Huon Pines
And have them made into table legs.

Only a Knocker
Can stir the Government
And still vote for them.

Only a Surfie
Can loaf in the sun all day
And complain about sunburn.

Only 'one of the blokes'
Can say: 'Owshegoin cobsy?'
And be understood.

Only an Aussie
Can be all these things
And not know it.

Heath Barrett, aged 15
Scottsdale High
Scottsdale Tas

1987

FAR HORIZONS

This year the competition received financial assistance as well as endorsement from the National Australia Day Council. For the first time printed entry forms were distributed in which sponsorships were acknowledged. Participation by children in isolated areas increased and through the various Correspondence Schools, entries were received from pupils in unusual locations, including one from a light house and one from a cruising yacht sailing around Australia! A generous private donation enabled a new prize to be added: The Lois Winter Dean Memorial Prize for isolated children.

Several poems were entered by Hibiscus High School in Papua New Guinea.

In total 1200 young poets expressed their view on the subject 'Far Horizons – Australia's Future seen through young eyes', a topic chosen to tie in with the Bicentennial year and taken from a line in the poem, 'My Country'.

Once again the influence of the media was evident especially in the Secondary Section where the majority of poems expressed disillusionment and hopelessness: 'there is no future for us' . . . 'the Bomb' . . . 'pollution' . . . and so on. Though pupils in the Primary Section voiced the same concern, their work showed more liveliness.

The Judges selected the winning poems 'on the basis of originality, structure and felicity of expression'.

Many encouragement prizes were sent with the reports and certificates to award worthy efforts.

SECONDARY SECTION

FIRST

Far Horizons

The deep thudding of distant bomb testing
Could be heard,
As they burst through the orange clouds of morning.
Their vapour trails pulled strands
Like stretched elastic.
The five jets split
And the formation shattered,
As a huge crack followed them
Across the sky.

The sun was a fading globe in the west —
And its reflection
Filled red, the dusty atmosphere.
A slow haze
Crept across the land.
And from the homestead
A gentle glow rose on the horizon
Near Roxby Downs . . . .

Katie Gardiner, aged 15
Woodlands CEGGS
Glenelg SA

PRIMARY SECTION

FIRST

Far Horizons

And the wild child wondered
As he turned his eyes to the west
And the far horizon,
What the future would hold
For this tribe of old:
These descendants of the Sun.

And thousands of years have come and gone;
Battles lost and battles won;
Each descendant improving his lot by law;
Laughing at those who had gone before.
Now videos, computers, spaceships and greed
Replaced the simple man and a simple need
To survive.

And as the spaceship left with the last of our race,
To find a new home in the realms of space —
One turned his eyes to the west and saw
The ghost of the wild child
On the far horizon.

Jodie Gill, aged 11
Logan Village State School
Logan Village Qld

Jodie in 1987

UNDER EIGHT SECTION

MY FUTURE

When I'm old and wrinkly
Too old to work
Too old to play,
I'll just stay inside
Watching TV all day.
Sometimes people will visit,
Not usually.
I'll be sad
I'll be lonely.
When people visit often
I'll be happy.
When they visit,
They tell me about when they were young.
I'd like to be able to watch cartoons
So I'll remember when I was young.
Young kids will be rushing to school
Visiting the moon,
Dropping notes back down
To friends on earth.
Space flying, watching monitors.
I'll be too old
Too old and too tired
To care
To share.
I'll just remember.
Please remember me.

Luke Schubert, aged 6
Comboyne Kinder
Comboyne NSW

PRIMARY SECTION

FAR HORIZONS

A little seed floated down to the moist soil.
Tell me who can tell me, will he grow
Or will he fail?
Will he get to see the city from his branches
High above?
Will the birds nest in him? Magpie? Turtle Dove?
Do you think when he grows tall, the woodsman
Will cut him down?
Along with all the other trees to make room
For city and town?
Yes! He'll see a far horizon.
He'll see a jewelled sea.
He'll see the magpie and turtle dove.
Or maybe even me.

Marnie Skillings, aged 11
Woodburn Central
Woodburn NSW

PRIMARY SECTION

Far Horizons

Australia's future through my worried eyes
On far horizons imperilled, lies.

Black against white, festering racial tension —
Friendship, trust and brotherhood could end such dissension.

Charred, barren country-side, smog filled air —
Or crystal clear waters, environmental care.

Nuclear nightmare, lawlessness, crime —
Or peaceful coexistence, love, justice sublime.

Worship the mammon, avarice, greed —
Or the poor and homeless from crisis freed.

Computerized technology, torment or treasure:
Downgrading the workman — or more time for pleasure.

Dollars buy forests, God's handiwork razed —
Or farmed commercial timbers, rainforests saved.

My country's destiny, jewel of all lands,
Lies precariously balanced in my hands.

Daniel Bolam, aged 12
St Therese's School
Edmonton Qld

LOIS WINTER DEAN MEMORIAL PRIZE

FAR HORIZONS

I look at the places
Where I play —
I wonder if my children
Will see it this way?

In places, man has
Chopped down every tree.
Chemical waste,
Dumped into the sea.
City air,
Full of pollution.
In the future
Will they find a solution?

Will there be robots
On call?
Will people find
Any jobs at all?
A robot Queen
And Prime Minister . . .
To me the idea
Seems quite sinister.

Perhaps the Super Powers
Will declare a war.
That would be the end of us
For sure.
Radiation
In the air.
Bombs and missiles
Everywhere.

Could we learn to live
In another place?
Perhaps with Martians
In outer space?

Dear God, please look down
On this earth,
From Salvador
Right through to Perth.
In every land
On every shore,
Please keep us safe
For ever more.

William Bowes, aged 10
School of the Air
Mt Isa Qld

SECONDARY SECTION

ADVANCE AUSTRALIA

Advance? Australia?!
Come off it, love, fair Dinkum.
What us Aussies is not doing is advancing
Any more than that cissy Capper's playing footy.
Come off all this *come on*, garbage
And perhaps we'll get there.

I mean, *come on*'s a bit passé what ho —
Like me French?
What we need is to stop coming
And start getting.

Achievers, that's what we need.
Oh yes, they're out there all right, love.
All these new-fangled, examination-type school-kids,
Learning heaps more than the 3R's —
That's what we learnt in MY day, love.

And kids don't just play games no more:
They go to some whopping institute in Canberra
To LEARN it.
All these 'versities and colleges and
I DON'T KNOW WHAT ELSE.

All them achievers, coming out into Australia
Makes me true blue 'eart bleed,
So it does.

Still, truth is, I liked it better when
Oz were just a backwater,
Abos was Abos,
Wimmin was wimmin,
Kids was kids
And real men didn't eat that French stuff —
What's it called?
Oh yeah.
Quiche!

Justine Bashford, aged 16
St Peter's Collegiate Girls
Stonyfell SA

Dorothea Mackellar Memorial Poetry Competition

GRANNIE AWARD

When I'm Older

When I'm older —
I hope
Our houses will still have
Yards for children to play
Under the sun
Or at the beaches.

When I'm older —
I hope
I can be a ballerina
And dance and make
People smile and
Give me flowers.

When I'm older —
I hope
I can help some children
In other poor countries
Who will die
From no food.

When I'm older —
I hope
I still remember
How lucky I am
To live
In Australia.

Jasmine Weeden, aged 5
Distance Education Centre
Charters Towers, Qld

UNDER EIGHT SECTION

Far and Close Horizons

Richard in 1992

The Horizon I can tell you,
Is a funny thing you know:
You never seem to get to it,
No matter how fast and far you go.
It's not like a turning road,
When you come to and see the bend:
A horizon simply stays ahead,
It seems to have no end!
But one thing I can really say,
I know you'll find this right:
The horizon comes in terrible close
On a dark and stormy night . . .

Richard Gudgeon, aged 7
Gulgong Public School
Gulgong NSW

1988

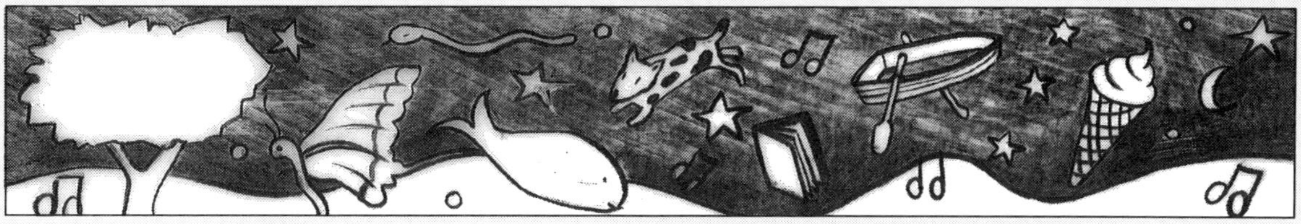

THE THINGS I LOVE

The competition was granted the status of a Bicentenary Event and the popular green and gold logo appeared on all 3260 Certificates sent to the 520 participating schools. The project received another grant from the National Australia Day Council, whilst the Executive Director of the NSW Australia Day Council came to the rescue, sharing the task of contacting all Heads of Education Departments with a request for dissemination of the 20 000 entry forms!

The set subject – 'The Things I Love' – was treated with gusto and optimism, offsetting the sombre thoughts expressed the previous year, when the children seemed to think that civilisation was on a path to disaster. This year there was a far more positive response to the theme: rainbows, football, flowers, vegemite, parents, ice-cream, God, Australia, brothers and sisters were all firm favourites!

Correspondence Schools' students sent their contribution from as far away as The Solomon Islands, Vanuatu and Spain.

Poems selected for final judging were again kept aside, to be given further consideration for the possible publication of an Anthology.

SECONDARY SECTION

FIRST

I LOVE . . .

A Sunday in summer,
the sun warms the corrugated iron roof,
rusted with time.

Shadows land on the verandah,
wooden floorboards supported on stumps;
a breeze passes under the house.

Peeling lattice wood
fences in the verandah;
ivy and fern cling.

Terracotta path tiles
lead to the gate;
a picket fence.

A timber house
amongst fields of tall
ripe, golden brown wheat.

Up the geometric stairs,
wooden and hollow;
made of teak.

Four poster bed,
soft; covered with mosquito net
high off the floor.

Stained glass windows;
stencilled ceiling;
polished wooden floor.

Silent starry night,
clear and still;
turn off the oil lantern on the table.

Kerri in 1988

Kerri Williams, aged 16
Concord High School
Concord NSW

PRIMARY SECTION

FIRST

THE THINGS I LOVE

These things I love:

Trees with long strong branches
holding the clouds in the sky;

Mountains so still
as if they were in a picture;

Cobwebs making curtains
for the dull grey moon;

A kite diving
looking for its prey;

A colour in the rainbow
helping to build the arch;

Dust sweeping
and making tiny patterns;

The breeze
diving in and out of the trees;

Lying in the grass
listening to native's stories;

Rocks telling the waterfall
to stop and not fall down the cliff.

City lights
calling for help;

The sun
talking to the world;

A frog's chest
pounding with the rhythm of the breeze;

A horse
kicking the ground like an enemy;

Clouds propped up on a hill
like pillows;

Flames prancing in the fire
like fairies;

Bellbirds
chiming in with the wind . . .

These things I love.

Ruth Lindsay, aged 8
Byabarra Public School
Byabarra NSW

Ruth in 1992

GRANNIE AWARD

THE THINGS I LOVE

I love porridge on a cold winter's morning
With lots of sugar and milk;
I love school and reading all sorts of books;
I love to play with my sister in our cubby house:
We pretend we are horses or a little mouse.

I love riding with Daddy on his motor bike.
We go mustering cattle, but not at night.
I love Nana, she is lots of fun:
We play with her, out in the sun.
I love my Mummy: she teaches me school
So I will not grow up to be a fool.

These are the things I love today.
Tomorrow they may be a different way.

Sasha Lindsay, aged 5
Distance Education Centre
Charters Towers Qld

PRIMARY SECTION

WHALES

It swims, as gracefully as a whispering cloud
Until they come. The silent whirring of the propeller makes it look.
The men have no mercy for the great thing.
It surfaces, breaking the glass of smooth lapping waves.
Droplets of warm water are forced out of a small hole.
And the merciless men fire their killing machine.

Michael Dean, aged 11
Morisset Primary
Morisset NSW

DOROTHEA MACKELLAR · Memorial Poetry Competition ·

LOIS WINTER DEAN MEMORIAL PRIZE

THE THINGS I LOVE

I love to see the sun rise
On an icy winter morning —
And watch the wildlife slowly wake
To face a new day dawning.

I love to see a rainbow set
Against a clear blue sky,
The mist that swirls around the hills
And the birds that fly so high.

I love the peaceful silence
As day succumbs to night —
And the stars that shine so brightly,
Turning darkness into light.

I love to see the morning dew
As it sparkles on a rose
And hear my mother say 'I love you'
As she gently kisses my nose.

Matthew in 1988

I love to see the smoke rise
From our chimney, when it's cold —
And see a tiny helpless kitten,
When it's just a few hours old.

I love to see the goat kids
Playing games with one another —
And my life in the great Australian bush
I would not change for any other.

I choose to see the things I love
Not only with my eyes —
I'm listening now, as the gumtrees sway
Slowly . . . with deep sighs.

So much in life is taken from us
With so much we have to part —
But the memories of the things I love
Will forever live in my heart.

Matthew J Forno, aged 12
Secondary
Correspondence School
Brisbane Qld

SECONDARY SECTION

THE THINGS I LOVE

The taste of air,
The smell of warmth
And words to keep
And cherish;

The dew
On the grass with
The wake of light
And hopes that
Do not perish.

These are the things I love.

Seng Chan, aged 15
Peter Board High School
North Ryde NSW

PRIMARY SECTION

THINGS I LIKE

Things I like
You don't like
And things you like
Just don't suit me . . .
So all together things I like
Are things just meant for me!

Anne Priestley, aged 12
Quandialla Central School
Quandialla NSW

PRIMARY SECTION

I Love Vietnam

The war has begun.
The people hurried away.
I could see the people run.
The families board the large boats,
As I hear firing of guns.
Further and further the boats sail.
I see my country fade away
As I cling onto the rail.

Le Khanh Quach, aged 11
Lidcombe Primary School
Lidcombe NSW

PRIMARY SECTION

I Love My Old Friend, The Tree

Every day after school I go to see a friend.
She's a tree, an old wise tree!
You can see that she's old by her warts and by the hair.
And in that hair there are cobwebs and creatures great and small.
She loses her hair,
But first she changes colour.
And in some places she's bald.
She hasn't combed her hair for ages.
I talk a lot. She's not bored.
If I ask a question, she waves her hand.
She's got a tan.
A brownish, blackish tan.
I can tell she's one hundred and seven, by the rings she wears.

Peter Tichy, aged 11
Seven Hills West Primary School
Seven Hills NSW

PRIMARY SECTION

THE THINGS I LOVE

Some love the hustle bustle
Of the traffic in a tussle
And the crowded city shoppers
Scurrying to and fro.

I love the open spaces
And the quiet untroubled faces
Of my country friends around me
Having time to care.

I love the early morning
With the birds awake at dawning
To see the cattle in the fields
The sheep among the hay.

I love to go horse riding
See the rabbits out of hiding
My dog running beside me
Sniffing in the grass.

I love to play at games and sport
In competitions fairly fought
A slumber party, friends together
Whispering till dawn.

I love my family gathered round
Joy and laughter both abound
A rolling surf on a sandy beach
A summer holiday.

I love all the simple things
Music, dancing, butterflies wings,
Icecream, chips and chocolate blocks
A bag of sweets.

Let others in their cities stay
It's in the bush I like to play
Where nature shows me all her tricks
A magic world.

Erica Baxter, aged 11
Gunnedah Primary School
Gunnedah NSW

PRIMARY SECTION

I Love Tigers

Three little tigers
Neath a sky of blue.
One little tiger now
A rich man's rug . . .
Now there's only two.

Two little tigers
Sitting in the sun.
One a hunter's trophy . . .
Now there's only one.

One little tiger
Waiting to be had.
Oops! he got the hunter first!
Aren't you kind of glad?

Richard Fong Lim, aged 10
Parap Primary School
Parap NT

PRIMARY SECTION

The Things I Love

I love SNAKES, cause snakes are cool.
I saw one swimming through the pool.
The snake is a wrigglesome sort of a beast.
If he finds a mouse, he will soon have a feast!
They also eat lizard and eggs and frogs.
Some live in old rockpiles and some under logs.
Some snakes are long and tapered and thin —
Some snakes are fat and live under tin.
If you see a snake basking out in the sun!
Don't pick it up! It's better to run!
But if you stay quiet and still and calm
You can watch for a while . . . it will do you no harm.
But if you attack them, they will defend!
Which may bring our story to an unfortunate end.

Jimmy Hutton, aged 10
Leeton Public School
Leeton NSW

PRIMARY SECTION

THE THINGS I LOVE

Boats and trains;
Paper planes;
Sitting in the shade.

Big balloons;
Merry tunes;
Things that I have made.

Dogs and cats;
Pins on hats;
Things that I have found.

Dads and Mums;
Biscuit crumbs;
Holes dug in the ground.

Ice-cream cones;
Telephones;
Cymbals and a gong.

Plants and trees;
Eating cheese;
A poem and a song.

These are the things that I loved
From my cradle till today,
(since baby times and nursery rhymes)
Like a hungry horse loves hay.

Patrick Porter, aged 11
Parap Primary School
Parap NT

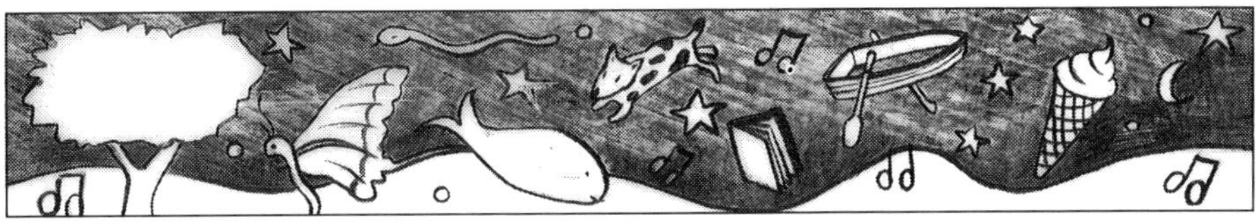

SECONDARY SECTION

HOME

As the stars become clearer
I can remember home.

The cool, prickly air before sunrise.
Sweet wafts of newly cut hay
Swirling about me as I waltz
Along the milky-smooth stone verandah.
It is cool beneath my feet:
A stark contrast
To the familiar blurry heat rising before me.
It distorts the nodding heads
Golden and heavy with grain.

I often find myself
in a place where the first thing you see
is the horizon
And the last bite of your apple tastes like the first.
I had not noticed,
But the constant 'swish' of the triticale
had become a roar.

Now, as the bright yellow lights crawl over the horizon
I hope the wisteria will be blooming
next time.

Wendy Sharpe, aged 15
Annesley College
Wayville SA

PRIMARY SECTION

LOVE FROM HEAVEN ABOVE

On the top of Heaven
There is some love.
It floats across the sky.
When we want it
It floats down.
There is so much love . . .
We can love too.

Lee Davy, aged 8
Glen Innes Infants
Glen Innes NSW

PRIMARY SECTION

THE TASTE OF NATURE

Hail, cold, slippery, melting on my tongue.
Burning sun, freezing sea.
Head through the waves and
Salt sliding down my throat.
Fresh picked strawberries and tickling champagne.
Spitting out cherry pips on a hot summer's day.
Icy watermelon, sticky water
Trickling down my arm.
Puppy on my pillow, tugging at my hair.
Crimson, royal blue rosellas,
Emerald king parrots with fire on their crowns.
Fire finches and blue wrens,
Tongues of fire and water.

Marguerite Angelides, aged 10
Sacre Coeur College
Glen Iris Vic

1989

Colours

The continued growth of the competition was again sustained through the National Australia Day Council's sponsorship and a record 5300 poems were received on the topic 'Colours'. By now, the competition was being referred to as 'Australia's leading poetry contest'! The names on the still hand-written certificates reflected the changing composition of our country's population, with surnames ranging from two consonants to a mixture of fifteen letters!

Competition judges Rosemary Dobson AO and Joan Phipson, retiring after six years of dedicated involvement, conclude in their report: 'We were most impressed with the standard of work. Though the majority of entrants resorted to a presentation of a list of coloured items, many poems were spontaneous, imaginative and original. Some showed genuine poetic feelings – whilst others were carefully constructed and intelligent . . .'

Several spectacularly presented school entries were received for exhibition on Australia Day and during the Poetry Festival in Gunnedah, which was held for the first time as part of the Dorothea Mackellar Anniversary Celebrations.

SECONDARY SECTION

FIRST

COLOURS IN THE LOLLYSHOP

On boot leather brown shelves,
stand ice blue crystal jars:
filled with rainbows.

A mosaic of bo-beeps,
liquorice twirls: southern sky black.

Watercoloured lollypops,
mint leaves: emerald.

A kaleidoscope of jelly beans,
coconut ice: fairy floss pink.

Opal coloured jelly babies,
honeycomb: wine yellow.

Carnival coloured popcorn,
milkbottles: vanilla white.

Jelly snakes: the colours of parrot fish,
bananas: lemon rind yellow.

Freckles appear as multi-coloured confetti,
butterscotch: tawny brown.

Red ruby toffee apples stand up-ended,
the blobs of colour are gay and joyous:
into paper bags, the colour of breadcrumbs.

Kerri Williams, aged 17
Concord High School
Concord NSW

Kerri in 1992

PRIMARY SECTION

FIRST

THE GREAT WHITE SWAN

The great white swan
swims slowly down
the wide blue lake;
on it a frown.

It bows its head
and slowly glides;
its movement slow,
it turns its side.

Above the sky
the grey clouds blow;
the great white swan
hides its head low.

Bright lightning strikes,
the sky turns black;
the great white swan
turns its white back.

Tamara Wakefield, aged 12
St Martins Lutheran Primary School
Mt Gambier SA

GRANNIE AWARD

COLOURS

Stacey in 1992

Yellow is the colour of the whipping sand.
Blue is the singing sea.
Red is the towel that dances in the wind.
Purple is the beach umbrella making shade.
Green is the grass up on the hill.

Stacey Lawson, aged 7
Boronia Park Public School
Gladesville NSW

LOIS WINTER DEAN MEMORIAL PRIZE

COLOURS

Black is the space in my mind.

A child's lonely cries surround me with blue.
Soft sounds of a flute: lilac drifts in.
Sunset at day's end: pink streaks by.
Rain on cut grass: green slips in.
Smoke in the air: grey attacks.
Icecream: splashes of white.
Cabbage drowns me in brown.
I stroke my cat: a golden glow washes over me.

Black is a space in my mind
waiting for my senses
to create the colours of my world.

Jasmine Weeden, aged 7
School of Distance Education
Charters Towers Qld

COLOURS

God had a paintbox,
And He brought it to Australia.

Up along here:
a sunny blue brushstroke
wanders across the sky.

The barren earth,
rusty, ancient:
a touch of red.
'That'll do nicely!'

A flourish of green
tipped with gold:
wattles cling to the rock
in desperation.

'Now,' God said, 'for the hard part.'
Two colours left:
Black and white.

So He took His brush and painted them
standing together
on the land —
His people:

One proud black nation,
then He painted a proud white nation.

He then handed to them His paintbox,
and He said:

'Go forth and paint your land.'

AND THEY CHOSE RED.

Michelle Hamill, aged 16
Sacred Heart College
Newtown Tas

SECONDARY SECTION

Colours June 4,1989

Orange the sun hung in the sky
White the clouds rolled in its hue
High were the spirits
At the demonstration:
Young ones, ripe for Liberty's colours.
Dank, dull green — Army's insignia.
Flames explode
From the rifles
Of the men;
Each wore the colour
Of Hate in his eyes.
Clashes of red and green
As tanks crushed thin tents.

'Pile up the dead.
Douse them with petrol.
Let the fierce flames of the
Human barbeque rage.
Coal up the fire!
Throw more students on!'

Black, the smoke rose high in the air.

Grey, the day
the People's Army killed.

Dark red spilled
All over the Square.

Extinguish the candle of hope . . .

Matthew Reekie, aged 14
Mount Carmel High School
Varroville NSW

COLOURS CONDEMNED

Thousands die feverishly:
Black Death.
Witches chant devilish tunes:
Black Magic.
The sun does not shine:
The world is cold:
Black Friday.
Vile letters disclosing dark secrets,
Demanding money:
Black Mail.
Cruel unfeeling,
Cold and merciless:
Black Hearted.
Illegitimate selling,
Sly swindling:
Black Market.
Scoundrel, non-conforming, rebellious:
Black Sheep.
The sign of pirates,
Villains of the sea:
Black Jack.
Created by God,
Crucified by your colour:
Black Man.

Anna Raptis, aged 16
Woodlands CEGGS
Glenelg SA

PRIMARY SECTION

THE HILL

Take me up to the top of the hill
Where the grass is ever so green,
And everything's more beautiful
Than anywhere else I've been.

Take me up to the top of the hill
Where the yellow daisies brightly glow,
Where the world seems so much more at peace
Than anywhere else I know.

Take me up to the top of the hill
Where the blue clouds and pink skylarks play,
So I'll remember everything
When I've grown old and grey.

Melanie Brown, aged 10
Wesburn Primary School
Wesburn Vic

UNDER EIGHT SECTION

COLOURS

The sun is yellow
With a duck inside,
Shining down on
the green sea.
On the blue deck
Of the grey ship
Sits an orange cat
On a pink chair,
Steering his way
To Queensland.

Rebecca Urquhart, aged 7
Curlewis Public School
Curlewis NSW

1990

COMING HOME

After the 1989 deluge of entries, schools were requested to conduct their own 'in-house' competitions and to submit a selection of no more than three poems per hundred pupils enrolled. This further enhanced the quality of the work and kept numbers down to a manageable level - 400 Schools from all over Australia (including Dauan Island State School via Thursday Island) entered a total of 3500 poems. The publicity surrounding the 75th Anniversary commemoration of the ANZAC landing in Gallipoli no doubt contributed to the surprisingly high number of 'Coming Home - from War' responses to the topic. Love for parents, the country, appreciation of nature, care for the victims of floods and concern for the environment were often expressed, especially in the work of younger students. Some harsh versions of either real or imagined situations involving abuse, drugs, streetlife and so on also emerged. On the whole, the reaction to 'Coming Home' proved to be thought-provoking.

New judges on the panel were poet/author Kate Llewellyn, best known for *The Waterlily* and English born Barbara Ker Wilson, esteemed author/editor. They found their new task both interesting and daunting. This was reflected in their first report in which they stated 'we were delighted to find so many expressions of genuine emotions and strongly felt experiences put into verse - without using cliches or doggerel rhythm and rhyme. Especially the work by younger children was spontaneous and uninhibited. Older students seem to become self-conscious and less likely to write original work, often lapsing into imitation. However, the long list of 'Highly Commended' and 'Commended' entries in all categories reflect the abundance of talent in our schools, obviously encouraged by dedicated teachers'.

The distinction 'First in the State' for Primary and Secondary Sections was introduced and High Commendations for quality of school submissions also received mention in the report.

SECONDARY SECTION

FIRST

Coming Home

She said it was not the way to leave . . .
Blank walls, cold hearts, empty smiles.
Flowers wilt in the sunshine,
Fish sleep eternally in the sea.
Grandma wants laughter, roast dinner,
Mud on her feet.
She is coming home
To die.

Rani Fisher, aged 16
Cairns State High School
Cairns Qld

Rani in 1990

PRIMARY SECTION

FIRST

I AM A PIGEON

I am a pigeon,
Getting ready for a race,
The club, home,
And the ring on my leg.

I am being let out,
Flying around,
The club, home,
And the ring on my leg.

I am flying for home,
And a hawk swoops down.
The club, home,
And the ring on my leg.

The hawk swoops down,
And tears open my crop.
The club, home,
And the ring on my leg.

Flying while losing blood,
My destiny in sight.
The club, home,
And the ring on my leg.

On the pen roof,
I'm in the trap.
The club, home,
And the ring on my leg.

The ring on my leg,
It is in the clock.
The club, home,
And the ring in the clock.

Two months later,
My crop is restored.
The club, home,
And the ring, now lost, and gone.

Robert Scealy, aged 11
Tamworth Public School
Tamworth NSW

GRANNIE AWARD

Coming Home

Kalo in 1990

Across the roof,
Under the fence,
Through the grass,
Up the steps,
Down the hall,
Across a room,
In the basket,
Home sweet home,
Purr, purr.

Kalo Tufui, aged 6
Gumdale State School
Gumdale Qld

LOIS WINTER DEAN MEMORIAL PRIZE

The Horses Are Coming Home

See the horses coming home, galloping down the track,
See the prancing stallion urge the foals on at the back.
Feel the mud hit your face from under flying feet,
Feel the sticky sweat drip in the early morning heat.
Taste the thick red dust as it fills your mouth and nose,
Taste the sweaty air as the leading stallion slows.
Smell the grassy sweetness as the horses snort and stare,
Smell the rich aroma of the fresh dung in the air.
Hear the thundering hooves as they whirl into their pen,
Hear excited voices call: 'They're all at home again'.

Christy Brown, aged 7
School of the Air
Broken Hill NSW

SECONDARY SECTION

COMING HOME

It was the summer of 'sixty-nine
When mother crossed the Greek borderline,
Her dejected eyes were full with tears,
For she was leaving home.

There was no fruit from the mountainous sand
So she sought some bread in the southern land,
With a woeful heart she left the shack
For her new wide barren home.

Today not only has she bread,
But a world of luxuries instead.
But she remembers in ages past,
The Hellenic shack called home.

So she packs her things and boards a plane
She heads for childhood's memory lane.
She longs to see the trembling shack,
The place that once was home.

But when she steps on the ancient soil
She seems to remember the sweat and toil,
For she's standing on the old infertile farm . . .
The farm she still calls home.

As she walks again on her childhood earth
In mainland Greece; her place of birth,
She sees that no-one's there for her
And she knows it's not really home.

She loses her love for the rocky nation
And while she sees Australia without elation,
She still heads for the southern, barren land
And she knows she's coming home.

Jim Douros, aged 14
Mentone Grammar School
Mentone Vic

SECONDARY SECTION

COMING HOME

Brown mouse
Coming home,
Whiskers stiff and straight.
Brown shiny coat,
Not a hair out of place.
Skittling, scuttling from here to there.
Darting, dodging, he must be aware
Of all the dangers that hide out of sight.
He looks softly round to spy an attack.
Those few, few seconds may save his life.
Every day.
Every night.
Preying.
Being preyed upon.
His house is in sight.
The door nicely hidden,
Unseen for the spinifex grass.
The hot desert sun rains hard on his back.
One quick dash and he's safe.

Meegan Kepert, aged 12
Darwin High School
Darwin NT

PRIMARY SECTION

COMING HOME

Where waves of the Bay of Bengal crash,
Lies my lost home — my Bangladesh.

With beautiful plains and raging seas,
Vast grasslands and many trees.

Flowing rivers, gentle breeze,
My love for you will never cease.

I think of you by night and day,
And end my verses as I say:

Where waves of the Bay of Bengal crash,
Lies my lost home — my Bangladesh.

Mumu Rahman, aged 10
Newton Primary School
Hectorville SA

PRIMARY SECTION

GOING HOME

Going home from school,
My bag is heavy.
My mind is tired.
My tummy is empty.

My mum is at the gate:
A smile.
A cuddle.
A kiss.

Home at last!

Melena Rigg, aged 8
Moil Primary School
Darwin NT

PRIMARY SECTION

COMING HOME

The band appeared.
The people cheered.
Our soldiers marched to war.

Men fought, some died,
Under a foreign sky.
Ten years struggle to survive.

No band appeared.
The people only jeered.
Our war weary soldiers returned.

No heroes among them.
No greetings for them.
Not welcome in their home land.

No band appeared.
The people still jeered.
They hung their heads in shame.

Then in '87 a whisper spread.
They were doing their duty.
They should feel no blame.

The band appeared.
The people cheered.
At last!
Our soldiers were coming home.

Jasmine in 1990

Jasmine Weeden, aged 8
School of Distance Education
Charters Towers Qld

SECONDARY SECTION

COMING HOME

I ask you nurse,
What's a war . . . without the death?
What's the Viet . . . without the Cong?
What's the M — . . . without 16?
Hey LBJ! . . . I've gone 'All the Way!'
Vietnam's a word . . . symbolizing death.
Especially when there's nothing . . . but a jungle wall,
To climb and kill, . . . to conquer all.
Hey My-Lai! Why were you there . . . for a Yankee barbarian?
Communism, Ha! A finer word . . . was never heard.
I turned 18 . . . in old Hanoi.
Hero I'm not, . . . but hell, can I fight.
Hey nurse, nurse! Won't you please?
tell my Mom . . . I'm coming Home.
I've done my time in Hell . . . and Heaven,
she's a-waiting for a vet from Vietnam.
My hands once gloves . . . of blue, white and red,
Now stained in the blood . . . of the dead.
A festered leg . . . sliced to the bone,
Kaleidoscope of pain, . . . a POW's nightmare moan.
Hey nurse! Please, nurse,
tell my Mom . . . I'm coming Home,
to Her,
a Heaven on her own.

Bernadette Johnson, aged 17
Terrigal High School
Terrigal NSW

1991

FRIENDS

Due to continued financial support by the National Australia Day Council (ADC) and direct involvement of all *ADC* Executive Directors, assisting with publicity and distribution of entry forms through the national network, participation nearly doubled in the States and Territories with 768 Schools entering a total of 4500 poems. Entries came from such faraway places as Norfolk Island, whilst the ages of contestants ranged between 3 (preschool) and 33 (re-entered High School student).

It was pleasing to note that the number of boys entering the competition was increasing! Also more High School entries were received than in previous years. Several Special Schools participated and remarkable work was received from integrated students. A poem in Braille was passed on to another blind participant.

The inaugural award for 'The Best Overall School Entry' was won by the Ursula Frayne Catholic College in WA, whilst the first prize for 'The Best Entry by a One-Teacher School' was awarded to Evesham State School via Longreach, Qld.

State winners were presented with a special trophy during Australia Day functions, held in the respective capital cities.

The judges reported 'the Subject "Friends" was interpreted in various ways; writing about human friends, young and old, imaginary friends, pets, teddy bears, even pianos . . . and a friendship between a spider and a ray of light. A number of poems showed a sense of humor and fun, whilst others dealt with tragedy and loss. Though we enjoyed the freshness and spontaneity of the younger entrants and often made allowances for age and lack of writing experience, we did feel that many of the older participants could have paid more attention to the form of their poetry. Sometimes - for example - a promising poem ended lamely . . . or embodied a good idea that was badly expressed. Many poems would have been more successful if more time had been taken over them. We would urge all young poets to read as widely as possible, both prose and poetry, and to strive for a voice of their own, based on individual observation - and **to read their work aloud** as a part of the process of composition'.

SECONDARY SECTION

FIRST

FRIENDS

Once,
sun shot through hot glass,
prisms on the ceiling
    rainbows playing in my eyes,
twisting in my seat with no escape.
cross,
    and then the rainbows were broken
and the sun was making freckles on your face,
freckles on my face
    burned my thoughts
and dried up your tears,
your gapped smile sat next to me.
I drew stickmen with hats
shady trees and shared a purple crayon;
You shared sticky chocolate,
grew taller than me and wrote left-handed
bumped my elbow all the time,
        but it did not matter:
I bumped yours back and teachers wrote
    what will we do with you?
Your mother laughed on the phone to mine.

Sun shoots through hot coloured glass,
staining my freckled face with rainbows,
unbroken rainbows that dance on the high arched ceiling
    tears on my face this time.

Felicity Glennie-Holmes, aged 17
Kooringal High School
Kooringal NSW

Felicity in 1991

PRIMARY SECTION

FIRST

My Friend And I

Once, when I was young
I made a kite with my friend.
We would buy the wood and the paper
And experiment to make the best kite,
My friend and I.

Once, when I was young
I flew the best kite with my friend.
We would hold the string with all our might
And feel the kite pull,
My friend and I.

Once, when I was young
Our friendship would fly as high as the clouds!
But sometimes, like a kite, it would fall
to the ground . . .
And then we would forgive and try again.
And then our friendship would again fly high,
My friend and I.

Vanessa Taylor, aged 12
Gunnedah Christian Community School
Gunnedah NSW

GRANNIE AWARD

I'M DRAWING A PICTURE OF MY PONY

I'm drawing a picture of my pony:
He's waiting for saddle-up time,
Supposed to be eating his porridge
Out of his own tin — all smelly and chewed.

I'm drawing a picture of my pony:
Coat like silver clouds —
Eyes like golden balls —
He always comes when I call.

I'm drawing a picture of my pony:
With ribbons around his neck
And trophy in my hand!
He's the best friend of all!!

Benjamin Clifton, aged 6
Tamworth Public School
Tamworth NSW

PAST FRIENDS

My friends, would you care to dance?
I can hear from the next room
the faint sounds.
The sounds of clicking heels, complementing
distorted tunes crackling out of the
old gramophone.
Through the next door I can see
Parading girls in tasselled skirts —
and around pale and slender necks,
chokers, studded with diamonds —
they're not real ones though.
Everyone knows that.
Each second, a parody of 1000 fluttering fake eyelashes,
like dark butterflies, settled
on wide and innocent eyes.

As the night wears on,
fanciful visions overflow from the minds
of every dancer — each intoxicated
with happiness.
The clock strikes eleven.
The dream sequence will soon be shattered.
No! Not yet! Just a while longer?
Ignoring the pleas
an intruder, dressed in white,
appears in the doorway —
blocks out the light.
I can't see them anymore. The dancing friends —
all gone.

Mr Johnson? Mr Johnson, there you are!
Daydreaming again were we?
It's time for me to change your sheets.
Come now, I'll wheel you out into the sunshine.
The pigeons are about.

No! Not yet! Please, just a while longer?
The night is still young!
Help me my friends. Save me.
The music is still
playing.

Zoe Ladyman, aged 16
Methodist Ladies' College
Claremont WA

SECONDARY SECTION

THE ULTIMATE FRIEND!

'Yes Sir! Can I help you?
You're looking for a friend?
Well, you've certainly come to the right place.
But could you be more specific?
The term "friend" is rather broad.

We have a wide variety to choose from.
For example we have the life-long loyal type;
Then there are the short-term companions.
We also have goody-goodies and know-it-alls!
Plus we have the type you can boss around
and dominate.

Have we found the right one yet?

Are you looking for a best friend?
They, I must admit, are very few in stock;
Or just the type for a bit of a rage?
They come in bunches and can be bargained for.

Oh, don't worry! we can debate on the price later.

If you'd be so kind as to look through our catalogue,
I am sure there is one for you!

By the way. Is that cash or Bankcard?
They don't come cheaply, you know.'

Erem Aziz, aged 15
Fahan School for Girls
Hobart Tas

SECONDARY SECTION

For You

For you
I would stop swearing tomorrow.
For you
I would do something really brave,
Like swim across the Pacific . . .
Or pat a cobra.
For you
I would climb Mt Everest,
Cross the Sahara,
Go to the dentist,
Drag my nails down the blackboard;
Watch you surf all day;
Listen to the Highway.
Sometimes I think I would even
Watch Channel Two
For you.

Catherine Piergrosse, aged 15
Christian Community College
Portland Vic

PRIMARY SECTION

Such Is A Friend

Such is a friend
As honey to a bee,
Teeth to a gum

A teacher to a pupil
Peas to a pod,
Milk to a cow
Corn to a cob.

All are important
All they need,
Having a friend
Is like water to a seed.

It will grow if you feed it.
It will die if you don't,
The less you do
The more it won't.

Michelle Place, aged 12
Port Augusta West Primary School
Port Augusta SA

SECONDARY SECTION

FRIENDS

Each day I relive the nightmare.
Hear their cries of terror.
See again the upturned dinghy;
Two white faces dragged under
By murderous, black currents.
Feel the floating fishing line —
A serpent twisted round my legs,
Playing me like a fish against time.
Brush that cold, fleeing fingertip
That vanished in the night.
Scream into darkness.
No answer. No fight.

Each day I gasp for more breath,
To plunge those inky depths . . .
To reach my drowning friends.

The pain never ends.

James Henderson, aged 14
Cairns State High School
Cairns Qld

SECONDARY SECTION

FRIENDS

Two new buddies,
shy and bewildered.

Two girls giggling
behind cupped hands.

Two matriarchs
sit knitting, watching,
While . . .
two old mates
gabble like geese.

The ageless and priceless
value of friends.

Paul Miller, aged 14
Mercedes College
Springfield SA

SECONDARY SECTION

FOREVER FRIENDS

The hot summer sun
Beats down mercilessly
On two golden heads,
Bent close together.
Quiet words pass between them.
Giggles dissipate
In the still, stifling summer air.

An iceblock drips,
Held between them.
Shared, like their words.
Can thought be shared?
It would seem so,
As the pair sit silently . . .
Staring up at the clear azure sky.

Lying side by side on dusty grass,
Neither can feel uncomfortable.
Though few words are exchanged,
Nothing is left unsaid.

They are
Forever friends.

Kimberley Clayfield, aged 13
Annesley College
Wayville SA

SECONDARY SECTION

As We Were Friends

How could you!
You never even said goodbye.
Leaving me here
to pick up my life
as if nothing happened.

Perhaps we were different.
I always told you everything.
Yet you never told me
of your intended departure.
You hid it from me
behind that sarcastic,
smiling face of confidence.

How could you!
You gave up so easily.
You let it steal your body,
never fighting it.
Eventually it stole your soul.

How could you
have acted as if nothing was wrong!
You said dreams never came true,
but told me to keep on dreaming.
I never understood
what you meant.
Until now!

That advice is always
in the back of my mind.
When I question your ways,
I start to understand
that you only evaded the truth
to spare me the pain.

How could you!
— Quite easily . . .
— As we were friends.

Narelle Hendrie, aged 17
Westminster School
Marion SA

(This poem was written with my friend in mind. We grew up together in the confines of the Adelaide Children's Hospital, where we clung to the hope of survival. Only she never lived to tell the story.)

In Choir I Sing Freedom

Stalling on my way to school,
Slowly eating away my sandwich,
Hoping no one will question me.

I am laughed at,.
Pointed at,
Left alone
In misery.
Emptiness breaks my heart.

Dragging my bag.
The smell of work
like ink spilled
on fresh paper.

The bell rings.
My thoughts explode
into a thousand directions.

Will I know what is 1 add 1?
Will Social Studies be hard?
Will I break a test tube
and spill chemicals on the floor?

In choir
it is all there.
Clear words in black and white.
Slowly we learn the words together.
Slowly we learn the tune together.
We sing
together.

In choir I am not alone.
In choir
I sing freedom.

Marijana Vlahov, aged 14
Ursula Frayne Catholic College
Victoria Park WA

JUST BE BEAUTIFUL

'Just be beautiful' he said,
'And be my pretty girl.
Don't worry about what I do
Or what's going on in the world.

Just buy your pretty dresses
With hems above the knee —
And paint your lips and eyelids
And let your hair hang free.

Don't worry about your beliefs
Or hide your head in a book.
Don't bother about speaking up,
I'm happy just to look.

Don't listen to what I'm saying
When the other guys are around:
You know I'll never mean it,
It's not the way that I sound.'

'I'll always love you' he said —
And these words echoed in my mind
Everytime he laughed at me
When he thought I was far behind.

'You should always be with me'.
His words resounded loud
When I saw him kiss that other girl
Across the noisy crowd.

His face was calm when I entered.
Never a stir or a sigh —
And I was careful not to show
The tears I had yet to cry.

'I've found another pretty girl'
I heard his smooth voice say.
'We can still be friends', he said —
But I had walked away.

Susan Holden, aged 15
Indooroopilly State High School
Indooroopilly Qld

ROSIE

They reckon it's time that old Mac left the bush,
He's been long enough way out west.
He'd be better in town, where it's cooler and clean —
And Rosie could have a good rest.

He leans on a gatepost and thinks for a while
of his land . . . and the homestead so cosy . . .
He recalls all the things he has done in the past —
But was it all fair to his Rosie?

All the jobs they have done; the fences they checked;
the stockwork they've shared in hot weather;
that rogue dingo that cut a wide swath through his flock —
He and Rosie had trapped him together.

And the 'sixties bad bushfire that near sent him broke:
The big one, that killed all the cattle . . .
He nearly gave up then, but fought it all through —
'twas Rosie who helped in the battle.

But now he is old and his hearing is bad;
His headaches are making him dreary.
That pain in his chest is his heart wearing out —
And Rosie looks tired and weary.

But would he be happy to leave his bush home,
Forget about marking and branding?
He could live in a unit . . . just down from the beach —
Surely Rosie would be understanding.

He could take in the parties, the places in town . . .
'though maybe he wouldn't fit in there . . .
Coz his favourite place is this mulga gatepost —
With a smoke and old Rosie . . . his mare.

Rebecca Brown, aged 13
Kinross Wolaroi
Orange NSW

SECONDARY SECTION

FREDDY FROG AND HIS FRIENDS

A little frog upon a leaf
Went sailing down the river.
His friends — all playing on the bank —
Saw Freddy shake and shiver.

He knew the river's waters fast
Would lead him to the sea . . .
'Jump! Jump! you silly frog!
It's easy as can be!'

'I can't! Can't!' he cried with fear
'I'm scared and I'm not clever!'
'You must! You must!!
Make haste: it's now or never!'

A handsome swan, quite fond of frogs,
Came gliding close to catch him:
'A tasty morsel, I declare!'
And stretched his neck to snatch him.

Then Freddy knew he had to jump!
'I will NOT be his dinner!'
He flung himself into the air . . .
His leap — it was a winner!

'I can! I can!' he laughed with glee
And swam and swam delighted
Back to his friends upon the bank —
All dancing and excited.

Damien Teague, aged 13
Kingscliff High School
Kingscliff NSW

PRIMARY SECTION

THREE OLD FRIENDS

Three old men, walking in the
Misty morning.
Trudging across golden sand —
And throwing their lines out to sea.
They sit in silence as they always do . . .
Until they feel a tug.
They haul them up.
There they are:
Three fish
Lying on the dew kissed grass.
One blue —
The colour of rippling water.
One gold —
The colour of a rich king's cloth
And one silver —
The colour of a shimmering lake
In the early morning.
Then, collecting their catch,
They walk back to their warm houses . . .
Looking forward to bacon and eggs
for breakfast.

Ella Holcombe, aged 9
Whittlesea Primary School
Whittlesea Vic

PRIMARY SECTION

My Friend

The wind is my friend.
My friend whistles to me,
Strokes my head as I'm resting —
I love wind.

The wind: it's a mother to me.
The wind rocks me when I'm tired.

Wind.
When I'm sad, I talk to you.
You listen to me,
Every word I say.

Wind, blow with me
Till I rest in peace.

Jessica Allaway, aged 10
St Mary's Primary School
Darwin NT

UNDER EIGHT SECTION

My Hermit Crab

You can be friends with anything,
Anything you wish:
You can be friends with a cat or a dog . . .
But could you be friends with a fish?

I am best friends with a shellfish!
He lives inside his shell
And looks out sometimes, as if to say
'Are you feeling well?'

He is red and pretty
And stays with me all day.
Even if he's lonely
He never goes away.

His sharp claws pinch my fingers
As if he's trying to talk!
I try to get his message
And take him for a walk.

Beth Moralee, aged 7
John XXIII College
Claremont WA

LOIS WINTER DEAN MEMORIAL PRIZE

FRIENDS

My friend is the Earth.
It needs a friend,
All alone in the
Blackness of space.

It shines out like a jewel,
With swirls of milky white
Over oceans of opal blue
That twinkle in the sun.
With a spark of desert red
And a flash of forest green,
All the colours of the opal
Can – with luck – be seen.

If we're not its friends,
If we don't care:
With its blanket torn away,
With its forests stripped bare . . .
As an empty arid wasteland
It will sadly fade away.

Yes! The Earth is my friend.
But some people just don't understand
That the Earth needs EVERYONE
To be its friend.
I am only one.

Daniel in 1991

Daniel Briffa, aged 10
School of Distance Education
Brisbane Qld

PRIMARY SECTION

FRIENDS

I have a friend who lives far away
I like to ring her but Mum says 'Pay'.
I write, she writes, I write back,
Why do I live so far outback?

My friend she visits on special days,
If only for a short while we get to play.
Treasures and secrets we share together,
Good friends, I hope, we are forever!

Margaret Bailey, aged 9
Evesham State School
Longreach Qld

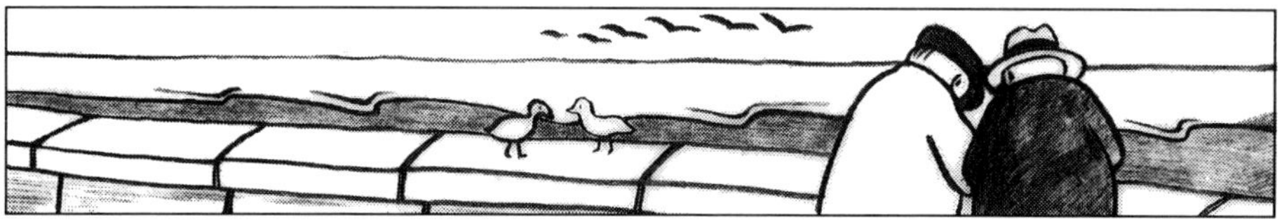

SECONDARY SECTION

Ode To A Forgotten Friend

At times when despair lay heavy across your youthful back —
and the ropes of life were pulled without an inch of slack . . .

During times of unjust punishment, when you had NOT done the
deed . . .
Through indignant cries of innocence that teachers would not heed,
his sympathetic ears were attendant; his silence would condole.
His boot button gaze held comfort and power to console.

He always seemed to be there, through times of guilt and sorrow.
A constant friend, who was here today and knew would be there
tomorrow.

But now you've grown older, wiser and your loyalties are deranged.
He lies forgotten on the rubbish heap.
It's not he, who's changed!
to be left there . . . abandoned . . . when the memories grow frail,
labelled 'Trash or Treasure' . . . at the churchyard sale.

Jane Instance, aged 15
Tangara School for Girls
Cherrybrook NSW

PRIMARY SECTION

Friends

Friends come fast,
Friends go slow,
At least I have ten friends, though.
Friends can be big or even small,
I don't care,
I want them all.

Tommy Pavlovic, aged 11
St Joseph's
Hindmarsh SA

1992

CHANGES

1992 turned out to be an exciting and fruitful year!

The 1991 State/Territory winners were presented with their awards at special functions, organised by Executive Directors of the respective Australia Day Councils. The Dorothea Mackellar Memorial Trust became an Incorporated Society - with modern headquarters, provided by Gunnedah Shire Council, furnished and equipped with the assistance of the National Australia Day Council and our new major Sponsor: QBE Insurance Limited. The Poetry Competition's growing importance as a cultural event was accentuated when the ninth National Annual Competition was officially launched by the NSW Minister for School Education and Youth Affairs - and similar ceremonies were conducted in other States.

For the first time, TAFE Colleges were invited to become involved, giving more mature students within the eduction system a chance to participate. In recognition of the efforts of dedicated teachers, who with apparent enthusiasm spent a great deal of time preparing their school's submission, a 'Teachers Appreciation Award' was introduced.

Another milestone was reached with the announcement that ABC Books would publish a selection of poems, entered in the Competition from its beginning in 1984 to 1992 inclusive. The chance to be included in this publication, proved to be quite an incentive! Promoted by Australia Day Councils, a record number of 860 schools participated this year. Again more inland isolated communities took part and entries were also received from surrounding islands as far away as Christmas Island.

Correspondence Schools always seem to deliver the unexpected . . . and through the West Australian Distance Education Centre, a poem was received from a student in The Netherlands!

Interpretation of the set subject varied as widely as distances crossed - and the following pages reflect part of the diversity of views expressed on 'Changes'.

SECONDARY SECTION

FIRST

THE OLD MAN'S KITE

She roamed gloriously
Amid summer skies —
A feather upon the wind,
Knocking on heaven's door.
Fluttering, weightless as a leaf,
Crimson, gold hues . . .
A stain on brilliant blue.

She roamed far and wide,
Curious as a child —
Seemed at times to want to reach the sun . . .
But all the while held firmly back
By an endless piece of twine.

And as the sun fell, so did she —
Gliding, gliding . . .
Coming to rest on the cool grass
To be picked up by her maker.
Back, as on every dusk, to collect her.
With loving eyes, that saw far more than
The bamboo and silk.

Gisela Pineiro, aged 17
Mary Mackillop College
Wetherill Park NSW

SECONDARY SECTION

CHANGING WAR SOUNDS

"whoosh" went the arrow,
"Clash" went the sword —
In a war long ago.
"Crack" went the rifle,
"Ssss" went the gas —
In a war some time ago.
"Chat chat" went the machine gun,
'Kaboom" said the grenade —
In a war a short time ago.
"Click" goes the button —
Silence. Desolation. Devastation.
So reads the plot of the war tomorrow.

Anne-Marie Kerr, aged 13
Mount Carmel College
Sandy Bay Tas.

DOROTHEA MACKELLAR Memorial Poetry Competition

PRIMARY SECTION

FIRST

AN AUTHOR FOR EVERY SEASON

(The Author changes with the Season)

The fog quietly settles in our gully:
A blanket concealing early morning secrets.

The last raindrops reluctantly releasing
Their grip on the dark green leaves of the old gum tree.

The lawn's blades glisten in the morning dew.

Winter, a mysterious Agatha Christie.

Wattles in bloom, cheering with their pom-poms,
The bottle-brushes' red cones feeding tiny birds.

The lavender perfume over-powering —
Small aphids chase each other in vivid roses.

Dashing foxes lunging through waves of grass.

Spring, a much loved, action-packed Enid Blyton.

Olive trees burn a haze over our gully.
The fierce blazing sun stewing unpicked apricots.

The hard, dry earth: creviced grandmother's skin.
Kookaburras squat sluggishly on phone wires.

Our grey cat drowses on the faded deck.

Summer, a soporific Beatrix Potter.

The brown grasses moan in the vicious wind.
The rolling clouds extinguish the life from the sun.

Cold, young goats huddle against their mothers.
The maple leaves quietly wither and turn to dust.

Lorikeets secluded in hollow trees.

Autumn, an unfulfilled, dying Charlotte Bronte.

Jessica Webster, aged 12
Mercedes College
Springfield SA

SECONDARY SECTION

A Cuddle Changes Everything

When I was younger,
Problems were different.
Bruised knees, a lost tooth;
Would Santa remember my list?
Every problem could be solved:
A bandaid, a cuddle, a story in bed.
That's all that was needed,
Before it all changed.

Now that I'm older
Problems have changed.
Along with exams and getting a car,
There's also a boyfriend.
Valentine's Day means more than birthdays.
Jeans made way for taffeta and lace
at the Senior Ball.
But problems are still solved by a cuddle.

The world's changing too.
The air is more polluted
And so is the sea.
Giant pandas and elephants may soon disappear.
A finger could still press that terrible button.
We must embrace the world
Before it all changes,
Changes forever.

Clare Fenton, aged 17
Ursula Frayne College
Victoria Park WA

PRIMARY SECTION

Changes

The moon rises up.
My blood churns thick.
My eyes pop out
And my brain goes "click".
I start to grow fur . . .
My nails grow long.
I howl like a wolf
In uproar and song
As the clock strikes twelve
With a fearsome gong.
Two minutes later
I am a full beast . . .
Ready and waiting
For my Halloween feast.

Daniel Bateson, aged 12
Northbridge Primary School
Northbridge NSW

SECONDARY SECTION

CHANGES

Down at the camp,
Near the river damp,
People are cold.

The water is chilly,
The wind is blowing,
The kids are freezing.

Tin windbreaks warm us,
Bough shelters protect us from the fierce sun,
A big wood fire cooks our food.

Now we have our own land,
Bush land, clean land, foodland.
ALPURRURULAM.

Food, house, shower,
Office, store, power,
Clinic, school, water.

Cars for travelling,
Toyotas for hunting,
Trucks for working.

Alywarre people are happy,
Old people are happy,
We like our own land.

Ashley Toby, aged 12
Alpurrurulam Community School
Lake Nash NT

PRIMARY SECTION

A CHANGE IN PERSPECTIVE

I watch the homeless blokes
laugh and tell silly jokes.
The park gardener buys them pizza and beer,
And when night has finally fallen
and the guys have all stopped talkin',
The gardener across the park
Yells 'lights out' for a lark.

Iain Perkes, aged 11
Parramatta Marist Jnr
Parramatta NSW

SECONDARY SECTION

CHANGES

Ever heard of a sunburnt country?
Well not much of it remains;
You have to search from top to bottom
To find those sweeping plains.

The good old Aussie farmers
Got us through the Great Depression;
The big sheep and cattle stations
Now all lost in the recession.

What about the native creatures
That used to roam 'round free —
Now all trapped in foreign zoos,
Where you have to pay to see.

The enchanting northern rainforests,
Where birds twitter musical scores —
Now overcome completely
By the roaring of chainsaws.

The big old towering eucalypts
That once were everywhere —
Now rapidly disappearing,
It just does not seem fair.

Why don't we try to stop this?
Let's save our sunburnt land!
It's up to us to help it:
The future's in our hands.

Amanda Fuller, aged 13
Wanniassa High School
Wanniassa ACT

THE CHANGING QUAD

Tall, cold concrete walls staring
Over baring flashes of metal
And empty wooden seats.
Crude markings marring the bitumen —
And litter scattered everywhere.

Empty space.
All alone.
The silence never broken.
Noise contained in classrooms.

The electric buzzer sounds —

A hive of activity.
Yelling and screaming.
Snatches of gossip floating around,
Picked up by unknown listening ears.
People walking from the Canteen
To their respective bays,
Nearly getting hit by feral tennis balls
And flying food.
Teachers prowling for victims . . .
Finding only the occasional few.

A fight!
And everyone gathers.
But it is soon broken up.

The bell sounds.
A groan of mortal pain echoes around the area . . .
And then
Everyone
Is gone.

Lara Carle, aged 14
Belconnen High School
Hawker ACT

LOST

People look at me differently now.
They study my face for a sign
Of my disease.
They keep their distance
In case I breathe
Or cough.
And destroy their future for them.
Four little letters can stand for so much.
A for alone
I for ignorance
D for death
S for suspicion.
My life summed up.
Each new born baby is studied
For the right amount of fingers and toes.
Mine were all there.
They still are.
Each baby is considered perfect.
So was I.
Not now.
Now I am in debt to our society
For being allowed to stay on
And pretend I still belong.
I have rules placed upon my being.
I stand in the place of a murderer
And I stray past the boundaries.
I made a mistake.
Two in fact.
A blood transfusion.
I trusted people.
I'm different now.
I don't make mistakes anymore.
After all, life's too short.
Isn't it?

Karina Meppelink, aged 17
Cairns State High School
Cairns Qld

PRIMARY SECTION

Not Quite Picnic Weather

Sun shining, birds singing,
baskets full of food we're bringing.
Pack up the car, turn on the key,
reach the park: sangers for me.

Wind turns cold, clouds turn black:
weather's changing, better turn back.

Get back in the car, put into gear,
drive back to house . . .
weather turns clear.

David Salmon, aged 10
Temora Public School
Temora NSW

LOIS WINTER DEAN MEMORIAL PRIZE

Grandma And Me

When my Grandma was a little girl,
She wore dresses and plaited her hair.
She rode a horse to school
And would sit at her desk in a chair.

Her desk had a hole for an inkpot,
Which she used to dip her pen in.
She wrote with chalk on a slate
And would wait for her teacher to begin.

I do my school at home
And listen to School of the Air.
I can wear shorts if I want to.
I can differently style my hair.

Life has changed around Chinchilla.
I would rather live here now,
Because I have a computer . . .
And that's better than milking the cow.

Tegan Plant, aged 8
School of Distance Education
Charleville Qld

SECONDARY SECTION

OLD WAYS—NEW WAYS

Long ago my people went hunting.
By walking a long distance.
By paddling their dugout canoe.
They ate bush tucker and sea food.
They had no shop in those days.
Their clothes were made out of bark
from the bush.

BIG CHANGES CAME TO OUR PEOPLE
The Macassan people came here.
They brought us knives, axes and cigarettes.
They gave names for some Aboriginal people.
They left tamarind trees
Standing near the beach.
They make beautiful shade
for our people.

MORE CHANGES CAME TO OUR PEOPLE

The Missionaries came here.
They brought us good news about Jesus.
They gave us food.
They helped us to build houses.
They made us happy
in those days.

Stephanie Yiwarrarra, aged 17
Milingimbi CEC
Milingimbi NT

AN UNWANTED CHANGE

The slicing words plunge forward,
The argument's plan is alive,
I cover my ears to block it out —
But it cuts right through like knives.

I see my parents glare and steam,
Their shadows on the truthful wall,
Take even turns to . . .
Rise and fall, rise and fall.

My screams of fury are my loudest ever,
But they cannot silence theirs,
I storm into their room ready to fight,
But all I achieve are sorrowful stares.

"Your father and I . . ." my mother began —
Her teary eyes glistening bright,
"We've decided to get a divorce, you see,
Because all we can do is fight!"

I couldn't believe it! I wouldn't believe it
But the truth kept haunting my mind;
I'd have to choose to live with one —
The other a new home must find.

My whole life changed right then and there,
And I chose to live with my mother;
Before my Dad was about to leave —
We promised to still love each other.

Tara Hor, aged 11
MLC School
Burwood NSW

PRIMARY SECTION

CHANGE-IN THE TORRES STRAIT

Our grandfathers loved fishing
With their wooden canoes and vine from trees.
Their houses were built of coconut leaves.

What a change! Now we have dinghies
With motors, life jackets, navigation lights
To catch slippery turtles on moonlit nights.

Hooks, sinkers and plastic lines
Take the place of scraggy vines . . .

So times have changed for the best
In the Torres Strait I guess!

Maria Pearson, aged 12
Our Lady of the Sacred Heart
Thursday Island Qld

PRIMARY SECTION

WONDERFUL CHANGES

I am an egg —
and you will see
the changes that
occur to me.

When I'm cracked
I hit the bowl.
My yolk and albumen
start to roll.

Flip, whip, scramble and beat . . .
Now I'm put over heat.
Round and round.
I'm stirred the most . . .

Now I'm dropped
on buttered toast.

Elizabeth Hinde, aged 9
Tirranna Public School
Tirranna NSW

PRIMARY SECTION

WHAT'S MISSING IN THIS CHANGING WORLD?

As I look out my window
What do you think I see?
I see black.
As I walk out my door
What do you think I see?
I see red.
As I get off the train
What do you think I see?
I see brown.
As I wait at the Bus stop
What do you think I see?
I see yellow.
As I walk upstairs
What do you think I see?
I see grey.
As I sit at my desk
What do you think I see?
I see blue.
Black smog, red bricks, brown paving, yellow cars,
grey smoke, blue desks . . .
But never any green.

Zoe Sergejevs, aged 12
Annesley College
Wayville SA

PRIMARY SECTION

CHANGES: PRIMARY-HIGH SCHOOL

You have just finished Primary School.
You were the oldest —
Now the youngest.
The kids are big, strong and tall.
You're just small, alone and scared.
No more bossing other kids.
Much more homework and tests.
The teachers are mean and strict.
Remember to be quiet in class.
Don't call out.
Keep shut.
Listen and learn the rules
And you'll be fine . . . .

Brett Cornelius, aged 12
St Peter's School
Bedford WA

PRIMARY SECTION

CHANGES IN THE SKY

Moonlight is beautiful — with glitter in the sky.
The glitter shines like a puddle of sun.
The moonman fires glitter
As the night woman comes closer and closer . . .
Then the moonman stops firing glitter,
Because the night woman is beside him.

The glitter is now all over the sky.

Melissa Jeltsen, aged 8
Lismore Heights Primary School
Lismore NSW

UNDER EIGHT SECTION

Olympic Changes

First there was a block of land.
Then there was a stadium.
Now it's in Spain —
Just for you.
Running round the Olympic track —
Light the flame!
Watch the games begin.
Now it changes.
Watch them swim, run, jump and hop.
Watch them laugh and watch them cry.
Watch them win and watch them sigh.
Win or lose:
Happy in Barcelona.

Sarah Wright, aged 7
Melbourne Grammar
Caulfield Vic

Changes In The Sky

I looked out of my window one rainy day.
I had a big surprise:
The sun and the rain
Were out together . . .
And there in front of my eyes
Was a rainbow.

Sarah Hithersay, aged 5
Quintilian Primary School
Mt Claremont WA

Changes

Clay changes from blobs to runny mud.
Hawks grow wings and learn to fly.
Atom bombs change when they blow up.
Nets get big holes when sharks get in them.
Ghosts fly about and disappear.
Elephants grow bigger and bigger.
Scooters change when they get muddy.

Heath Lodge, aged 6
Gladstone Primary School
Gladstone Tas

PRIMARY SECTION

CHANGING HOUSE

We've lived in this house
For as long as I remember.
I don't want to move.
I'm going to be sad forever.

We're moving to a flat:
It's so so small.
My mother's angry:
She tells me not to bawl.

I dream I'm moving to a palace . . .
And then I'm not so sad —
But when I wake up
Again I feel pretty bad.

I guess you have to move sometimes;
There is nothing I can do.
I wonder which family will move into my house . . .
I really wonder who.

Noah Erlich, aged 10
Leibler Yavneh College Primary
Caulfield Vic

PRIMARY SECTION

CHANGE

Change . . . I hate it! it sits in my pocket like a lump of lead.
And when I want to use a public phone or get on the bus
I never have it.
Change bogs me down,
Making holes in my pockets
And change gets me nowhere.
I hardly ever have enough cash
And change
Just doesn't buy anything.

Chloe Hall-Brown, aged 12
Ashgrove State School
Ashgrove Qld

SECONDARY SECTION

UTOPIA: THE NORTHERN TERRITORY

The relentless heat,
bouncing off the tarmac into a billion pieces,
creates illusions of shifing dancers against the horizon.
The mulga tree —
cowed and crooked with its leaves like fingers,
points at the sky in lifelong quest for rain.
The fence posts —
sucked and buffeted by the roving sand,
stand like sentries: guards to the cattleman's fortune.
The ranges —
cathedrals of rock, enigmatic and repelling,
hide the paintings and memories of dreamtime.

The beer bottle
glints harsh and jagged by the roadside —
opiate of the Anangu.
Rightful owners of this arid Eden.

Zoë Beecher, aged 16
The Cathedral School
Hermit Park Qld

SECONDARY SECTION

POLLUTION

Tumbling waters rushing by —
Streaming down a mountain side.
Making its way to the winding stream
of flashing silver.
Shining liquid shadowed by buildings,
Channeled into tunnels.
A rampant spirit caged
and beaten by the unnatural.
Fattened by rubbish —
Pumped full of grime —
Choking the flowing waters.
Back to the ocean.
Dripping out a cement pipe.
A slow, sad trickle.

Nicole Stubbs, aged 15
Kaleen High School
Kaleen NSW

Dorothea Mackellar Memorial Poetry Competition

GRANNIE AWARD

My Station Is Big

My Station is big:
There is not enough bush tucker for me
To walk from one side to the other.

There are many birds that live here.
To me they sing their song.
Sometimes I sing along!

I sing of my hope for the rain to come,
Filling the dry creek again,
So I can splash and play in the water.

From the dust, dirt and ash
I would have the spear grass make a dash
For the clouds drifting by,
Tickling them on the underside.

I know too soon the grass goes brown,
Wind knocks it down.
The orange coloured flowers
of the Bloodgum, bloom.

Smoke floats by.
Fires crackle along.
The sun sets over my Station.

My Station is big.
Its edges stay the same,
But somehow in-side
Always seems to change.

Lily Teelow, aged 5
Katherine School of the Air
Katherine NT

TAFE SECTION

FIRST

PROGRESSION

When I was a child, I was afraid to drink milk because of Strontium 90.
And my Mother would say, "What do you mean you don't like it? Think of the children in Korea."
And I, with the fervour of youth chalked "Ban the Bomb" signs on the railway underpass and marched in spirit on Aldermaston.
Singing protest songs.
But the greenhouse effect was what happened to Uncle Bert's tomatoes.
When I grew up I was going to conquer the world.

When I was in my thirties I was afraid the kids would catch measles or weren't getting enough vitamins.
And I heard myself echoing, "Think of the poor starving children in Vietnam."
And they, with the fervour of youth, textered rude messages against the French at the bus-stop.
Singing protest songs.
And the greenhouse effect was still working on Great Uncle Bert's tomatoes.
As the kids grew up, I hoped they would conquer the world.

Now I am older than I want to admit and I am afraid the world has gone mad.
And I hear my daughter saying, "Eat your dinner. There are children starving in Ethiopia."
And my Grandchild with the fervour of youth, pickets
McDonalds, and reads spraypainted "Save the Whales."
"No more Chernobyls" on the expressway.
Singing protest songs.
And the Greenhouse Effect, Ozone Depletion is an everyday news item.
When she grows up there will be a world to conquer.
Won't there?

Wendy Boland,
Shellharbour TAFE
Shellharbour NSW

INDEX